Solve
Story Problems
Using Pictures

Grade 2

Carson-Dellosa Publishing LLC
Greensboro, North Carolina

Full Support

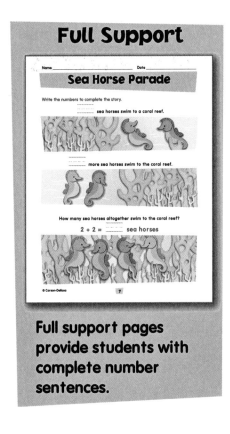

Full support pages provide students with complete number sentences.

Medium Support

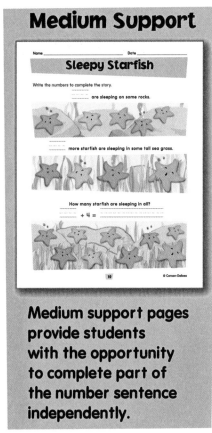

Medium support pages provide students with the opportunity to complete part of the number sentence independently.

Independent

These pages challenge students to write complete number sentences and solve them independently.

Credits

Content Editor: Karen Cermak-Serfass
Copy Editor: Rebecca Benning
Layout and Cover Design: Nick Greenwood
Cover and Inside Illustrations: Robin Bauer, Nick Greenwood, Julie Kinlaw, Ray Lambert

Carson-Dellosa Publishing LLC
PO Box 35665
Greensboro, NC 27425 USA
www.carsondellosa.com

Printed in the USA • All rights reserved.
1 2 3 4 5 HPS 15 14 13 12 11

ISBN 978-1-936024-16-2
335101151

Introducing: Solve Story Problems Using Pictures

Solve Story Problems Using Pictures is designed to simplify the often-challenging task of problem solving for young learners. As students immerse themselves in this playful, colorful, undersea world, they will learn basic facts using concrete and tactile methods of problem solving. Each story is sequenced in three illustrated frames. Students can count the pictures in each frame to find story problem solutions. Classroom manipulatives can also be placed on the pictures to provide extra support if necessary. Students will find this interactive method exciting and entertaining as their confidence increases and they master story problem strategies.

Solve Story Problems Using Pictures has been created for use by both classroom teachers and parents. This book meets the National Council of Teachers of Mathematics (NCTM) Number and Operations standards for second grade. It utilizes the Concrete-Representational-Abstract method to teach story problem solutions. It is an excellent resource for students and any child learning or struggling with story problems.

Skills Include:

- Addition Facts: 0 through 20
- Subtraction Facts: 0 through 18
- Multiplication Facts: 2 through 8
- Division Facts: 2 through 5

This book is a versatile tool to master basic math skills. Varied levels of number sentence support provide opportunities for differentiated instruction and flexible grouping. A reproducible Journal Template (page 5) has been included so that students can create their own math stories. Parents can use this book at home to reinforce basic facts and practice story problem strategies. This book's unique design provides all of the support needed for learning in the classroom and at home.

Table of Contents

Aquatic Addition

Facts 0 through 9

Seaworthy Sums

Facts 10 through 20

Deep Sea Differences

Facts 0 through 9

Even Bigger Fish

Facts 10 through 18

Marine Multiplication

Facts 2 through 8

Diving into Division

Facts 2 through 5

Name _____ Date _____

_____

Write your own math story! Write the number sentence. Solve the story problem.

_____

_____

_____

Name _____ Date _____

Swimming with Friends

Write the numbers to complete the story.

_____ whales are swimming to an island.

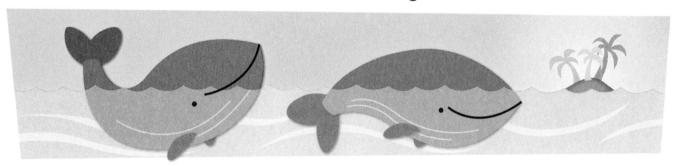

_____ more whale joins them along the way.

How many whales are swimming to the island?

2 + 1 = _____ whales

Sea Horse Parade

Write the numbers to complete the story.

_____ sea horses swim to a coral reef.

_____ more sea horses swim to the coral reef.

How many sea horses swim to the coral reef altogether?

2 + 2 = _____ sea horses

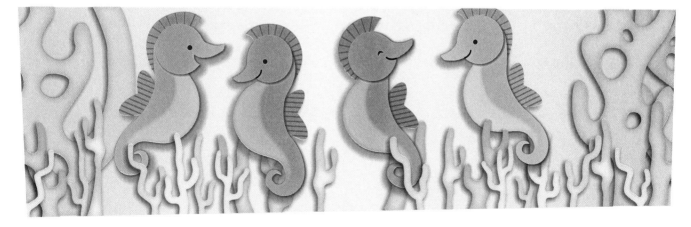

Singing Fish

Write the numbers to complete the story.

_____
_____ fish are singing around a coral reef.

_____
_____ more fish join them.

How many fish are singing around the coral reef in all?

3 + 2 = _____ fish

Name _____ Date _____

Sea Turtle Pals

Write the numbers to complete the story.

_____ sea turtle pals swim together.

_____ more sea turtles join the swimming fun!

How many sea turtles are swimming altogether?

4 + _____ = _____ sea turtles

Sleepy Starfish

Write the numbers and word to complete the story.

_____

_ _ _ _ _

_____ starfish are sleeping on some rocks.

_____

_ _ _ _

_____ more starfish are sleeping in some tall sea grass.

How many starfish are sleeping in all?

_____   _____   _____

_ _ _ _   + 4 =   _ _ _ _   _ _ _ _ _ _ _ _ _ _ _ _ _

Whale Watching

Write the numbers to complete the story.

_____ whale swims by a boat in the ocean.

_____ more whales swim by the boat.

How many whales swim by the boat in all?

_____ + _____ = _____ whales

Octopus Workout

Write the numbers and word to complete the story.

_____
- - - - - - -
_____ octopuses are working out near some rocks in the ocean.

_____
- - - - - - -
_____ more octopuses join the workout.

How many octopuses are working out in all?

_____   _____   _____ _____
- - - - - + - - - - = - - - - _____

Name _____ Date _____

Dancing Sea Horses

Write the numbers and number sentence to complete the story.

_____ sea horses are dancing in the waves.

_____ more sea horses join them.

How many sea horses are dancing altogether?

_____

Fish Like to Read

Write the numbers to complete the story.

_____ fish are reading.

_____ more fish decide to join them.

How many fish are reading in all?

3 + 7 = _____ fish

Sunning Sea Turtles

Write the numbers to complete the story.

_____ sea turtles are sunning themselves on the beach.

_____ more sea turtles join their friends.

How many sea turtles are on the beach?

7 + 6 = _____ sea turtles

Seaweed Swim

Write the numbers to complete the story.

_____ fish swim into the seaweed to play.

_____ more fish follow them.

How many fish are there in all?

$9 + 5 =$ _____ fish

Collecting Clams

Write the numbers to complete the story.

Sally Starfish finds _____ clams and puts them on a rock.

Later, Sally finds _____ more clams.

How many clams does Sally find in all?

2 + _____ = _____ clams

Owen's Stamp Collection

Write the numbers to complete the story.

Owen Octopus glues _____ stamps into his notebook.

Owen finds _____ more stamps to put into his notebook.

How many stamps does Owen have in his notebook now?

_____ + 8 = _____ stamps

18

Busy Hat Store

Write the numbers and word to complete the story.

_____
_____ sea horses buy hats from their favorite hat store.

_____
Later that day, _____ more sea horses buy hats.

How many sea horses bought new hats?

_____   _____   _____
8 + _____ = _____   _____

Turtle Tag

Write the numbers to complete the story.

_____
- - - - -
_____ sea turtles are playing tag.

_____
- - - - -
_____ more sea turtles join the game.

How many sea turtles are playing tag in all?

_____   _____   _____
- - - - -   - - - - -   - - - - -
_____ + _____ = _____ sea turtles

Tunnel Travelers

Write the numbers and word to complete the story.

_____
_ _ _ _ _ _____ fish swim through the tunnel.

_____
_ _ _ _ _____ more fish are waiting to go through the tunnel.

How many fish swim through the tunnel altogether?

_____   _____   _____   _____
_ _ _ _ + _ _ _ _ = _ _ _ _ _____

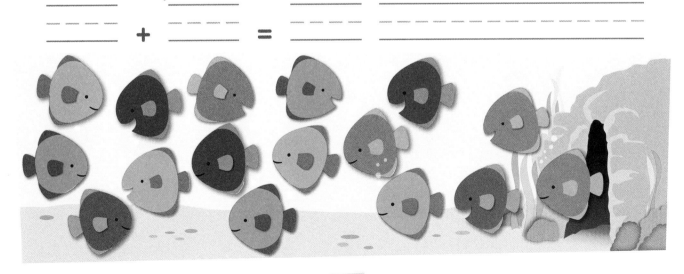

Counting Shrimp

Write the numbers and number sentence to complete the story.

William Whale counts _____ shrimp swimming in the ocean.

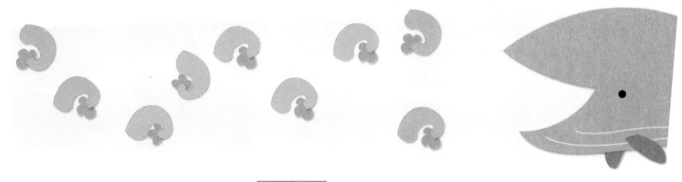

Later, William counts _____ more shrimp swimming by him.

How many shrimp does William count in all?

_____

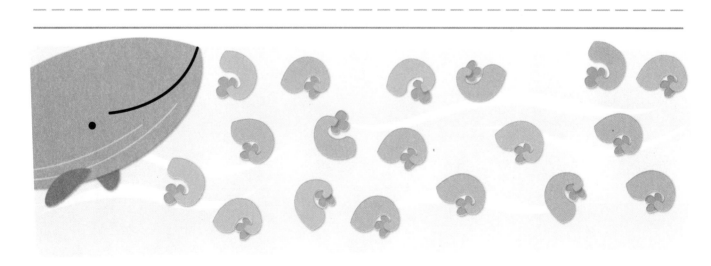

© Carson-Dellosa

Star Light, Star Bright

Write the numbers to complete the story.

Olivia Octopus counts _____ stars in the night sky.

Later that night, Olivia counts _____ more stars.

How many stars does Olivia count altogether?

5 + 15 = _____ stars

Name _____ Date _____

Stephen's Garden

Write the numbers to complete the story.

_____

Stephen Starfish plants _____ kelp in his garden.

_____

Then, Stephen plants _____ coral branches in his garden.

How many things does Stephen plant in his garden?

_____ + _____ = _____ things

Counting Coconuts

Write the numbers and number sentence to complete the story.

Wendy Whale sees _____ coconuts on the beach.

Wendy sees _____ more coconuts in the water close to shore.

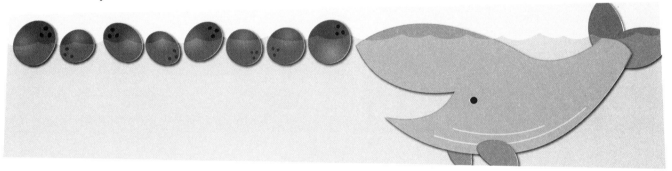

How many coconuts does Wendy see altogether?

_____

Napping Sea Horses

Write the numbers to complete the story.

_____ sea horses are napping in the sea grass.

_____ sea horses wake up and swim away.

How many sea horses are left napping?

4 – 2 = _____ sea horses

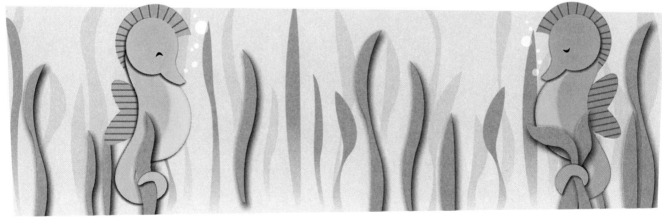

Sea Plant Park

Write the numbers to complete the story.

_____

_____ fish are playing on the playground at Sea Plant Park.

_____

_____ fish goes home.

How many fish are still at Sea Plant Park?

6 − 1 = _____ fish

Time for Tea

Write the numbers to complete the story.

_____
_____ lobsters are having tea.

_____
_____ lobsters leave when they finish their tea.

How many lobsters are having tea now?

_____
8 − 4 = _____ lobsters

Playing Ball

Write the numbers to complete the story.

_____ octopuses are playing baseball.

_____ octopuses have to go home.

How many octopuses are left playing baseball?

5 – _____ = _____ octopuses

Whitney's Gifts

Write the numbers to complete the story.

Whitney Whale has _____ gifts.

Whitney opens _____ gifts.

How many gifts does Whitney have left to open?

_____ – 3 = _____ gifts

© Carson-Dellosa

Reef Painting

Write the numbers and word to complete the story.

_____

_____ fish are painting.

_____

_____ fish decide to take a lunch break.

How many fish are still painting?

7 − 6 = _____ _____

Beach Ball Bounce

Write the numbers and word to complete the story.

Oliver Octopus is bouncing _____ beach balls.

Oliver lets _____ beach ball bounce away.

How many beach balls does Oliver have left?

q – _____ = _____ _____

Sea Turtle Sand Castle

Write the numbers to complete the story.

_____ sea turtles are building a sand castle.

_____ sea turtles go home.

How many sea turtles are still building the sand castle?

_____ − _____ = _____ sea turtles

Name _____   Date _____

Starfish Family Picture

Write the numbers and word to complete the story.

_____
- - - - -
_____ starfish are getting ready to take a family picture.

_____
- - - -
_____ of the youngest starfish swim away.

How many starfish are in the picture?

_____   _____   _____   _____
- - - -   - - - -   - - - -   - - - - - - - -
_____ - _____ = _____   _____

Wyatt's Toy Box

Write the numbers and number sentence to complete the story.

Wyatt Whale plays with _____ toys.

Wyatt decides to put away _____ toys.

How many more toys does Wyatt still need to put away?

_____

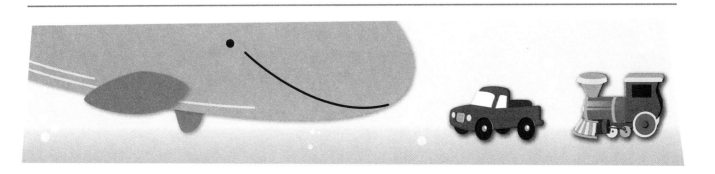

Sea Horse Races

Write the numbers to complete the story.

_____
_____ sea horses are in a race.

_____
_____ sea horses cross the finish line.

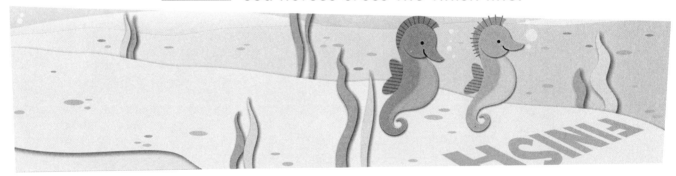

How many sea horses are still racing?

10 – 2 = _____ sea horses

Name _____ Date _____

Starfish Studies

Write the numbers to complete the story.

_____
_____ starfish are doing schoolwork.

_____
_____ starfish finish their schoolwork and go home.

How many starfish are left doing schoolwork?

11 − 9 = _____ starfish

Hide-and-Seek

Write the numbers to complete the story.

_____
little clown fish are playing hide-and-seek.

_____
little clown fish have to go home.

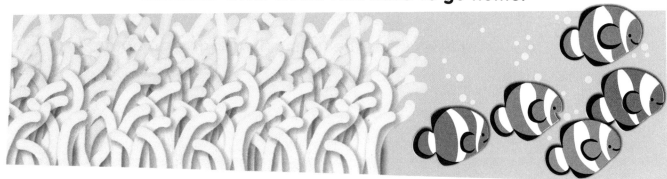

How many little clown fish are still playing hide-and-seek?

13 − 5 = _____ clown fish

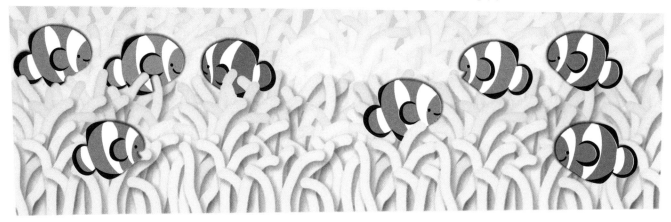

Ready to Write

Write the numbers to complete the story.

Sarah Starfish holds _____ pencils.

Sarah drops _____ of them on the way to the pencil sharpener.

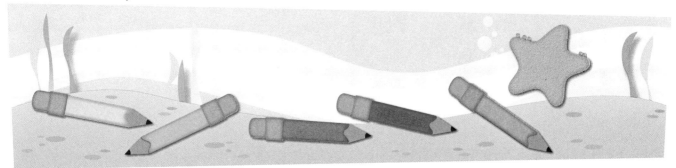

How many pencils does Sarah have left?

10 – _____ = _____ pencils

Whitney's Marbles

Write the numbers to complete the story.

Whitney Whale finds _____ marbles.

_____ of the marbles are yellow.

How many marbles are red?

_____ – 6 = _____ red marbles

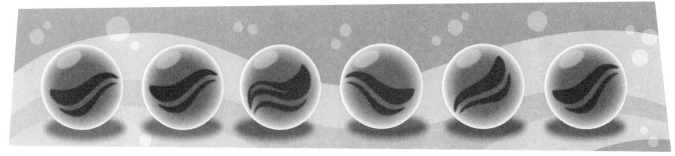

Playtime with Friends

Write the numbers and word to complete the story.

Sam Sea Horse plays with _____ friends in the ocean.

_____ friends swim away.

How many friends are playing with Sam now?

15 – _____ = _____ _____

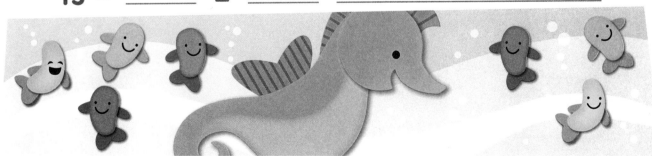

Going to the Movies

Write the numbers and word to complete the story.

_____

_____ fish are going to the movies.

_____

_____ fish change their minds and go home.

How many fish go to the movies?

_____ _____ _____

_____ – 9 = _____ _____

Orlando's Rings

Write the numbers to complete the story.

Orlando Octopus has _____ rings.

Orlando chooses _____ rings to give to his friends.

How many rings does Orlando have left?

_____ − _____ = _____ rings

Sean's Paint Job

Write the numbers and word to complete the story.

Sean Sea Turtle needed _____ cans of paint to paint his house.

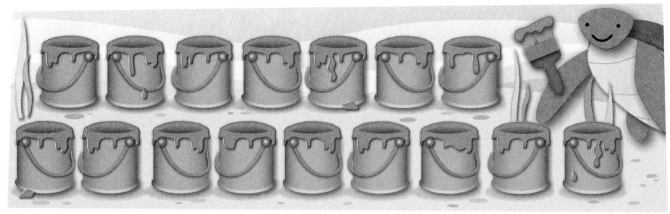

Sean uses _____ cans of paint.

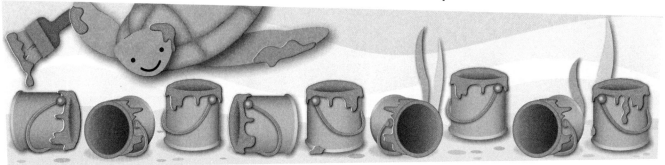

How many cans of paint does Sean have left?

_____ - _____ = _____ _____

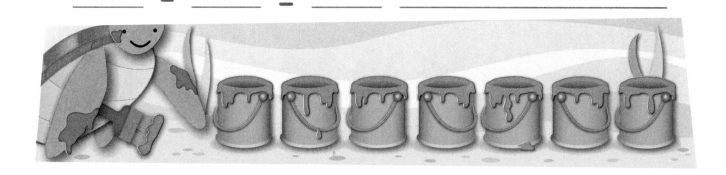

Name _____ **Date** _____

Fiona's Flowers

Write the numbers and number sentence to complete the story.

_____

Fiona Fish finds _____ flowers growing in the ocean.

_____

_____ of the flowers are anemone daisies.

How many of the flowers are shell tulips?

_____

_____

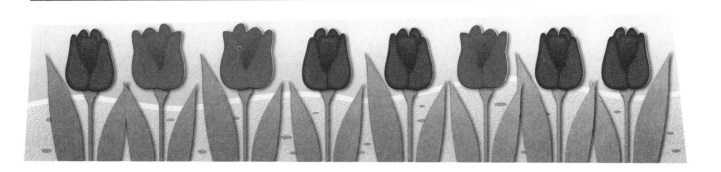

Name _____ Date _____

Show and Tell

Write the numbers to complete the story.

Forrest Fish shows his toy trucks. He shows his _____ blue trucks first.

Then, Forrest shows his _____ red trucks.

How many toy trucks does Forrest have in all?

2 × 2 = _____ toy trucks

Bookstore Turtles

Write the numbers to complete the story.

_____ sea turtles visit a bookstore.

Each sea turtle chooses _____ favorite books.

How many books did the sea turtles buy altogether?

$3 \times 2 =$ _____ books

Sea Horse Snacks

Write the numbers to complete the story.

_____ sea horses want an afternoon snack.

Each sea horse chooses _____ pieces of fruit.

How many pieces of fruit do the sea horses have in all?

$3 \times 3 =$ _____ pieces of fruit

Fancy Olivia

Write the numbers to complete the story.

Olivia has _____ long arms.

She puts _____ bracelets on each arm.

How many bracelets is Olivia wearing?

8 × 2 = _____ bracelets

Freddie's Rock Collection

Write the numbers to complete the story.

Freddie places _____ collection boxes in a row.

Freddie puts _____ of his favorite rocks into each collection box.

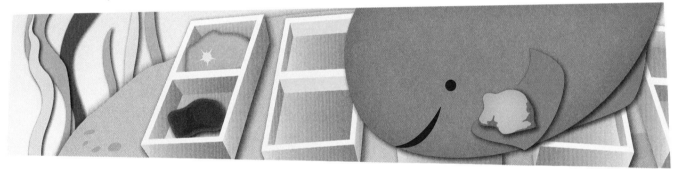

How many rocks does Freddie put into his collection boxes?

5 × _____ = _____ rocks

50

Seth's Favorite Treasures

Write the numbers to complete the story.

Seth Sea Turtle has _____ bags of treasure.

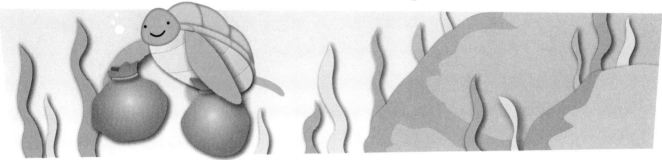

Seth removes _____ treasures from each bag and lines them up.

How many treasures does Seth have in all?

_____ × 4 = _____ treasures

Family Travels

Write the numbers and word to complete the story.

A family of _____ octopuses is going on vacation.

Each octopus decides to take _____ suitcases.

How many suitcases do they take altogether?

_____ × 3 = _____ _____

Lobsters' Lucky Finds

Write the numbers to complete the story.

_____
_____ lobsters are looking for shiny pebbles.

Each lobster grabs _____ shiny pebbles.

How many shiny pebbles do the lobsters find in all?

_____ × _____ = _____ shiny pebbles

Bags of Books

Write the numbers and word to complete the story.

Wendy Whale brings home _____ bags of books from the library.

Wendy takes _____ books out of each bag.

How many books does Wendy have altogether?

_____ × _____ = _____ _____

Fish Having Fun

Write the numbers and number sentence to complete the story.

_____
_ _ _ _ _
_____ fish want to juggle.

_____
Each fish gets _ _ _ _ _ balls.

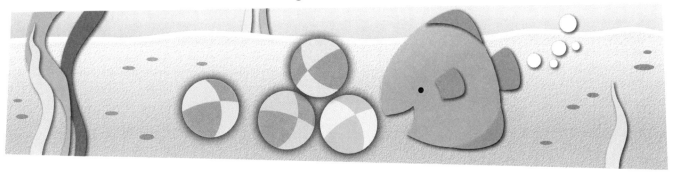

How many balls do the fish juggle in all?

_____
_ _ _ _ _ _ _ _ _ _ _ _ _ _ _ _ _
_____

Surfing Sea Horses

Write the numbers to complete the story.

_____ sea horses want to go surfing.

Only _____ surfboards are left to rent.

How many sea horses will ride on each surfboard?

4 ÷ 2 = _____ sea horses

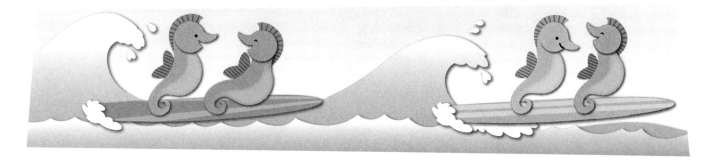

Sorting Shells

Write the numbers to complete the story.

Sarah Sea Turtle finds _____ seashells.

Sarah sorts the shells. She separates them into _____ equal piles.

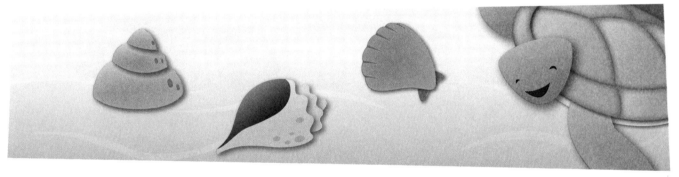

How many seashells are in each pile?

$9 ÷ 3 =$ _____ seashells

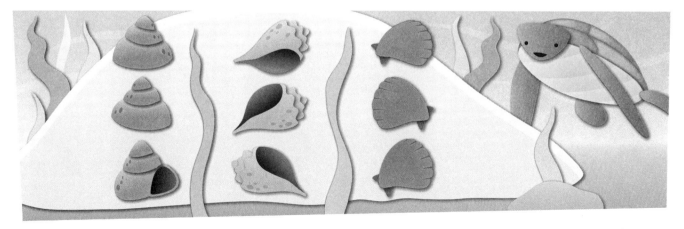

Lots of Lobsters

Write the numbers to complete the story.

Felicia Fish sees _____ lobster claws sticking out of some sea grass.

Felicia remembers that every lobster has _____ claws.

How many lobsters are hiding in the sea grass?

16 ÷ 2 = _____ lobsters

Counting Creatures

Write the numbers to complete the story.

Owen Octopus sees _____ bright eyes peeking out of an anemone.

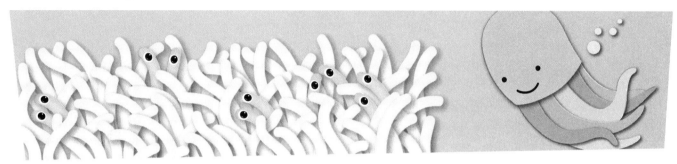

Owen knows that each creature has _____ eyes.

How many creatures does Owen see in the anemone?

$$10 \div \underline{\quad\quad} = \underline{\quad\quad} \text{ creatures}$$

Name _____   Date _____

Butterflies on the Beach

Write the numbers to complete the story.

Sasha Sea Turtle sees _____ butterflies fly over the beach.

Sasha watches them fly to _____ bushes.

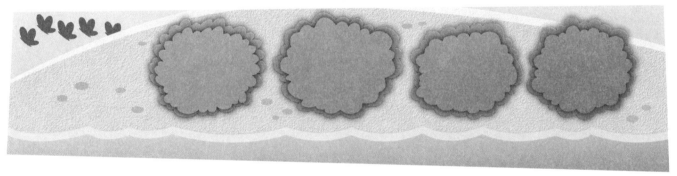

How many butterflies land on each bush?

_____ ÷ 4 = _____ butterflies

Rowing for Home

Write the numbers and word to complete the story.

_____

_ _ _ _ _

_____ lobsters relax on the beach all day.

_____

_ _ _ _

The lobsters have _____ rafts to get home.

How many lobsters ride on each raft?

_____   _____   _____

_ _ _ _ _   ÷ 3 =   _ _ _ _ _   _ _ _ _ _ _ _ _ _ _ _ _
_____   _____   _____

Dancing in Pairs

Write the numbers to complete the story.

_____

_ _ _ _ _ _

_____ fish are going to the dance.

The fish decide to dance in pairs of _____ .

How many pairs of fish are dancing together?

_____   _____   _____

_____ ÷ _____ = _____ pairs of fish

Name _____ Date _____

Starfish Family Garden

Write the numbers and word to complete the story.

The Starfish family buys _____ seed packets for their summer garden.

Each of the _____ family members plants the same number of packets.

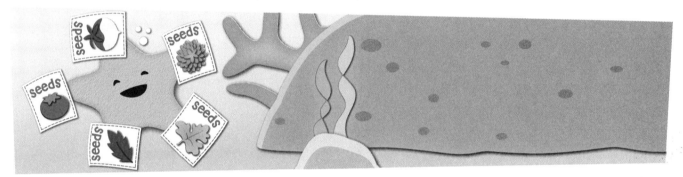

How many seed packets will each family member plant in the garden?

_____ ÷ _____ = _____ _____

Collecting Clams

Write the numbers and number sentence to complete the story.

Forrest Fish finds _____ clams.

Forrest will put _____ clams in each basket.

How many baskets will Forrest need for his clams?

_____

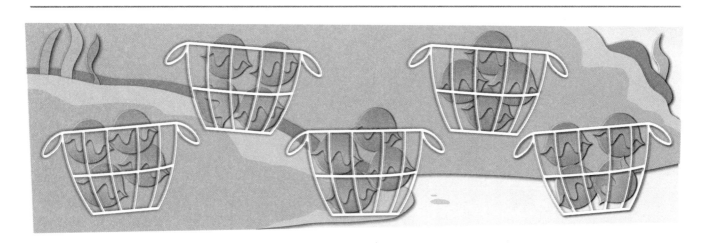